The Emancipation Proclamation

DAVID & PATRICIA ARMENTROUT

Rourke

Vero Beach, Florida 32964

www.rourkepublishing.com

PHOTO CREDITS: Cover image and Page 42 © Getty Images. Page 13 Courtesy of Images of Political History. Page 20 Courtesy of the Department of the Interior. All other images from the Library of Congress

Title page: *An optimistic vision of southern life after Lincoln's Emancipation*

Editor: Frank Sloan

Cover and page design by Nicola Stratford

Library of Congress Cataloging-in-Publication Data

Armentrout, David, 1962-
  The Emancipation Proclamation / David and Patricia Armentrout.
     p. cm. -- (Documents that shaped the nation)
  Includes bibliographical references (p.   ) and index.
  ISBN 1-59515-233-4 (hardcover)
 1. United States. President (1861-1865 : Lincoln). Emancipation Proclamation--Juvenile literature. 2. Lincoln, Abraham, 1809-1865--Juvenile literature. 3. Slaves--Emancipation--United States--Juvenile literature. 4. United States--Politics and government--1861-1865--Juvenile literature. I. Armentrout, Patricia, 1960- II. Title. III. Series: Armentrout, David, 1962- Documents that shaped the nation.
  E453.A76 2004
  973.7'14--dc22
                          2004014418

Printed in the USA
CG

TABLE OF CONTENTS

THE EMANCIPATION PROCLAMATION

On January 1, 1863, President Abraham Lincoln signed the **Emancipation Proclamation**. It was one of the worst times in American history—the Civil War. The document declared *"all persons held as slaves within any State or designated part of a State, the people whereof shall then be in rebellion against the United States, shall be then, thenceforward, and forever free."*

The Emancipation Proclamation is a little more than 700 words. However, the small section printed above explains Lincoln's intent. It means that all slaves, living in territory in rebellion against the federal government, were declared free. This area included states that had **seceded** from the Union in 1860 and 1861.

Lincoln's proclamation changed the course of the Civil War in many people's minds. It was also the beginning of the end of slavery in the United States.

President Abraham Lincoln

A. Lincoln.

ABRAHAM LINCOLN.
SIXTEENTH PRESIDENT OF THE UNITED STATES.

SLAVERY IN AMERICA

Several events in history played roles in the development of slavery in America. Europeans brought slaves to the first American settlements. In some cases, Native Americans were also enslaved. When the British

colonized America in the 1600s, they brought slaves over to help cultivate the land. These slaves were known as **indentured servants**. Some of these slaves were Blacks, but many were unemployed white Englishmen. Deceitful businessmen told them the New World was a place of opportunity. They were then "sold" under contract to American farmers.

In exchange for free passage to the New World, these slaves had to work for their owners for many years. At the end of their contracts, they would be given "freedom dues," such as tools, land, and a gun. Some slaves were freed, but others had their contracts extended indefinitely.

Many indentured servants enslaved by the British were non-Christians. They could be freed if they converted to Christianity.

An artist's impression of slavery in 1840s America

Male and female slaves are separated on board the slave ship Wildfire.

Slave trade in America began in 1619, when a Dutch trade ship brought Africans into Jamestown Colony. As new colonies were settled, more slaves were needed. The slave trade continued, and later it was legalized. No longer were these laborers indentured servants; they were legal property.

Many slaves attempted to run away. For whites, it was easier to escape to freedom because of the color of their skin. Many Native Americans made it to freedom, too. They knew the land and were able to hide from their owners. Blacks, however, had a harder time escaping. They were not familiar with their surroundings, and the color of their skin made them an easy target for capture.

By the 1800s, the North felt differently about slavery than the South did. The economy in the South was based on crop sales. In order for Southerners to make a profit, they needed to sell large quantities of crops such as tobacco and cotton. Southern **plantation** owners needed laborers to keep their fields planted and harvested yearlong.

Northerners did not need field laborers in order to keep their businesses profitable. The Northern states, heavily populated with European **emigrants**, established large cities with factories. The Northern economy was based upon the goods produced in factories, not farms.

Two slaves work cotton through a cotton gin.

The cotton gin, invented in 1793 by Eli Whitney, was a machine that separated cottonseed from its fiber. Its invention allowed the cotton crop to become profitable for Southern plantation owners.

THE MISSOURI COMPROMISE

In 1818, the Union had 11 free states and 11 slave states. The territory of Missouri **petitioned** to enter the Union as a slave state. A New York representative proposed an **amendment** to ban slavery in Missouri. State governments on both sides of the slavery issue bombarded the federal government. A **compromise** needed to be made.

Finally, in 1820, The Missouri Compromise allowed Missouri to enter the Union as a slave state, while Maine entered the Union as a free state. The compromise also stated that area north of Missouri would enter the Union as free territory. The area south of Missouri would be slave territory. The Missouri Compromise helped keep a balance of power in Congress.

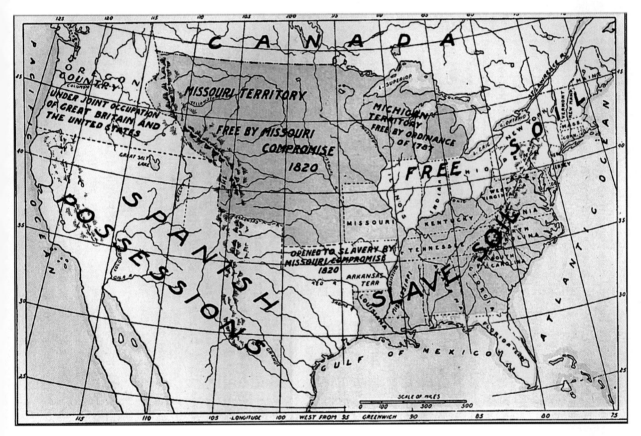

A map of 1820 showing free and slave territories

THE FUGITIVE SLAVE ACT

In 1850, Congress passed a combination of bills called the Compromise of 1850. The Compromise included the **Fugitive** Slave Act. The Fugitive Slave Act was a law that allowed slave owners the right to organize groups to search for, and recapture, runaway slaves. Fugitives and freed slaves, no matter where they lived, were denied the right to a trial by jury, and they were forced back into slavery.

The Act also required private citizens to assist in the recapture of fugitive slaves. If citizens were found helping runaways, they were jailed and fined and required to pay **restitution** to the slaves' owners.

Citizens shooting fugitive slaves—the effects of the Fugitive Slave Act

THE UNDERGROUND RAILROAD

Even though laws like the Fugitive Slave Act penalized people who helped slaves, they encouraged **Abolitionists** to fight harder to free slaves. After the law was passed, there was an increase of slaves escaping through the Underground Railroad. The Underground Railroad was a secret system of paths, trails, and homes that were used by runaway slaves. The "railroad" led slaves from the South into the North, including Canada.

Famous runaway slave and Abolitionist Frederick Douglass

Whites and slaves developed the Underground Railroad. Harriet Tubman was a famous "conductor" of the railroad. She was born into slavery in Maryland. She escaped slavery and went to Philadelphia through the Underground Railroad. Harriet Tubman made about 20 trips to the south, helping slaves escape. It is estimated that she led 300 slaves to freedom without losing a single "passenger."

Harriet Tubman led many slaves to freedom through the Underground Railroad.

THE KANSAS~NEBRASKA ACT

As U. S. territory crept westward, the slavery issue continued to cause tension between the North and South. Evidence of this occurred when Congress passed the Kansas-Nebraska Act in 1854. This law opened the Kansas and Nebraska territory to settlement and allowed the territories to decide if they wanted slavery. This angered Abolitionists in the North, as well as proslavery Southerners. People from all over the United States flocked to settle Kansas so their votes would be counted when the territory petitioned for statehood.

A sequence of violent conflicts between proslavery and antislavery activists took place in the Kansas territory between 1854 and 1856. These events, known as Bleeding Kansas, are believed by some to be the beginnings of the Civil War.

*John Brown, a violent antislavery leader, led the
attacks on proslavery men in Kansas.*

THE ELECTION OF 1860

The presidential election of 1860 was interesting, to say the least. Candidates were forced to take sides on the issue of slavery. The Constitutional Union Party, whose candidate was John Bell, said slavery should be left alone. The Democratic Party was split. Proslavery Democrats nominated John C. Breckinridge. Antislavery Democrats nominated Stephen Douglas.

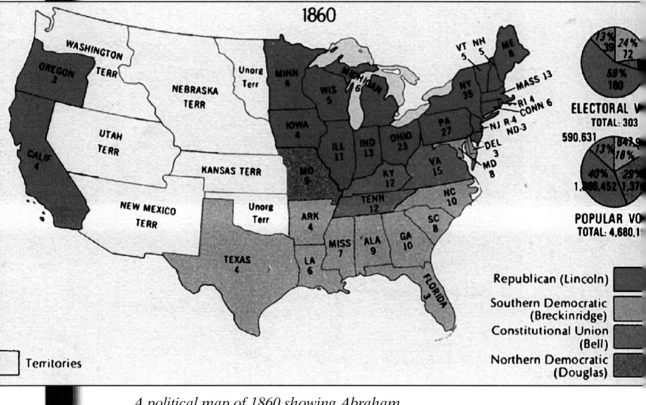

A political map of 1860 showing Abraham Lincoln winning the election

A portrait of Lincoln entitled "Our Next President"

The newly formed Republican Party, which firmly opposed slavery in new territories, nominated Abraham Lincoln.

On November 6, 1860, Lincoln won the election with both the electoral and popular vote, but he was anything but popular in the South. Lincoln's election to the presidency led directly to the separation of the Union.

The Constitutional Union Party was composed mostly of Whigs – a party formed in 1834 by those who opposed President Andrew Jackson's political policies. The last national election in which a Whig candidate ran was the 1852 presidential election.

SECESSION

Lincoln promised not to touch slavery where it existed. He told the South that he was only against slavery's expansion into new territories. The South, however, did not trust Lincoln.

South Carolina held a secession convention in Charleston. On December 20, 1860, South Carolina voted to secede. Six days later Federal soldiers moved in at Fort Sumter in Charleston Harbor. Under the command of Major Robert Anderson, they took control of the fort before South Carolina seized it. Then, Mississippi, Florida, Alabama, Georgia, Louisiana, and Texas seceded from the Union.

Fort Sumter sits on an island in Charleston Harbor, South Carolina.

In February 1861, the seceded states held a meeting in Montgomery, Alabama. They formed a new government called the Confederate States of America. Rebels began seizing forts and arsenals throughout the South. Meanwhile, South Carolinians had Fort Sumter surrounded with cannons, determined not to let any new supplies reach Anderson and his troops.

This wood engraving shows Confederate soldiers making camp in Texas.

FIRST PRESIDENT OF THE NEW SOUTHERN CONFEDERACY. — PHOTOGRAPHED BY BRADY.

Jefferson Davis was inaugurated president of the Confederate States of America on February 18, 1861. Lincoln was sworn in as the 16th president of the United States on March 4, 1861.

THE CIVIL WAR

Fort Sumter was surrounded by Southern troops for weeks. They requested Major Anderson's surrender, but he refused. On April 12, 1861, the South fired shots on Fort Sumter, and the Civil War began. Two days later the Union army surrendered the fort. When Lincoln got word of the surrender, he called for 75,000 volunteers to protect the capital. By the time summer arrived, four more states had left the Union: Virginia, Tennessee, Arkansas, and North Carolina.

A Union volunteer in uniform, with rifle, bed roll, and canteen

Union soldiers and a band march through a city on their way to join the Civil War.

However, four slave states remained loyal: Missouri, Kentucky, Maryland, and Delaware. These states were known as Border States because they lay on the border between the North and the South.

When Virginia left the Union, those living in the western counties did not want to secede, so they formed their own government and named their state West Virginia. West Virginia was the only state formed during the Civil War. It was admitted to the Union as the 35th state on June 20, 1863.

The battle at Fort Sumter was small compared to the battles that followed in the war's first year. By July of 1862, both sides had experienced heavy losses, and the Union had very few victories.

Lincoln continued to struggle with the issue of slavery. Before the war, Northerners had urged the president to abolish slavery, but if he freed slaves now, Northerners would think the war was about slavery and not about preserving the Union.

Lincoln worried about his army and the Border States. If he were to free slaves, soldiers from the Border States might leave the Union army and join the Confederate forces. The Union army could not afford to lose men.

The Battle of Fredericksburg, Virginia, left nearly 18,000 dead, wounded, or missing after this terrible siege.

Lincoln had been careful not to take action against slavery, but after a year debating the issue, it was time to free slaves. He wrote his Emancipation Proclamation.

On July 22, 1862, Lincoln met with his advisers to discuss measures that could improve the Union's position in the war. Lincoln read a part of his Emancipation Proclamation aloud and told his advisers that he wanted their opinion. Most of Lincoln's advisers were against the idea. They told the president to wait until the Union had a victory before announcing his plan for emancipation. Lincoln agreed to wait.

President Lincoln visits McClellan and other officers at the Antietam battlefield.

Major General George B. McClellan at the Battle of Antietam

On September 17, Union and Confederate forces fought a brutal battle at Antietam, Maryland. It was one of the bloodiest battles of the Civil War. When it was over, more than 25,000 dead and wounded lay on the battlefield.

LINCOLN'S EMANCIPATION PROCLAMATION

The Battle of Antietam was the Confederacy's first eastern attempt to invade the North. Neither army could claim a true victory, but the Union gained an advantage when the Confederacy withdrew their forces back into Virginia. The president had what he needed to move forward with his emancipation.

On September 22, 1862, President Lincoln read his Emancipation Proclamation to the public. This *preliminary* Emancipation was a direct order to the Army. The proclamation warned the southern states that if they did not return to the Union by January, all slaves would be forever free. Lincoln's proclamation also allowed former slaves to join the Union army.

Lincoln reading his first draft of the Emancipation Proclamation to his advisers

The Emancipation Proclamation caused mixed reactions in the North. Some whites thought the war was now being fought to free slaves. Others believed it was the greatest proclamation ever issued.

Abolitionists were angry because the proclamation did not include slaves in the Border States. Many people wanted Lincoln to take back the proclamation.

On January 1, 1863, Lincoln signed his Emancipation Proclamation. Southern slave owners did not free their slaves, but when slaves finally got word of the Emancipation, many fled north on their own, and some joined the Union forces. The Emancipation Proclamation did what Lincoln wanted. It helped free slaves, it caused the South to lose its laborers, and it increased the Union forces.

200,000 African Americans joined the Union forces by the war's end.

Black Union soldiers defended Dutch Gap canal in Virginia.

THE THIRTEENTH AMENDMENT

The emancipation of slaves did not end the war. Confederate troops continued to fight for their freedom, and Union troops continued to march south, liberating slaves. By the end of 1864, Union forces had captured Atlanta and Savannah in Georgia. To many, these victories meant the end of the Civil War was near.

Lincoln wanted to end slavery completely before the war's end, so he worked with Congress to amend the Constitution. On January 31, 1865, Congress voted and passed the Thirteenth Amendment, which made slavery illegal.

On April 9, 1865, General Robert E. Lee surrendered to General Ulysses S. Grant at the Appomattox Court House in Virginia. That surrender marked the end of the Civil War.

Union General Ulysses S. Grant served as the 18th president of the United States from 1869 to 1877.

General Lee and his army surrendered to General Grant on April 9, 1865.

THE LOSS OF THE GREAT EMANCIPATOR

President Lincoln delivered his last public speech on April 11, 1865. He addressed a crowd on the White House lawn. Lincoln spoke about how the government and military would work together to reconstruct the South. He said that everyone agreed that the seceded states were "out of their proper relation with the Union," and all should join in by "restoring proper practical relations between these States and the Union."

Three days later, President Lincoln and his wife joined some friends at Ford's Theatre in Washington, D.C. While sitting in a balcony watching a play, an actor named John Wilkes Booth entered from behind and shot President Lincoln in the back of the head. Booth escaped, but was found later by Union soldiers and killed.

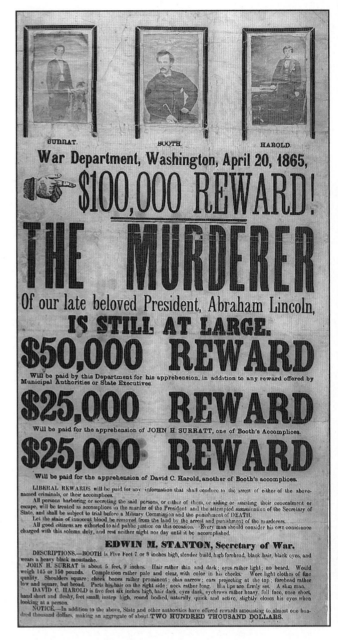

This poster advertises a reward for the capture of Lincoln's assassin.

A drawing of John Wilkes Booth shooting President Lincoln at Ford's Theater

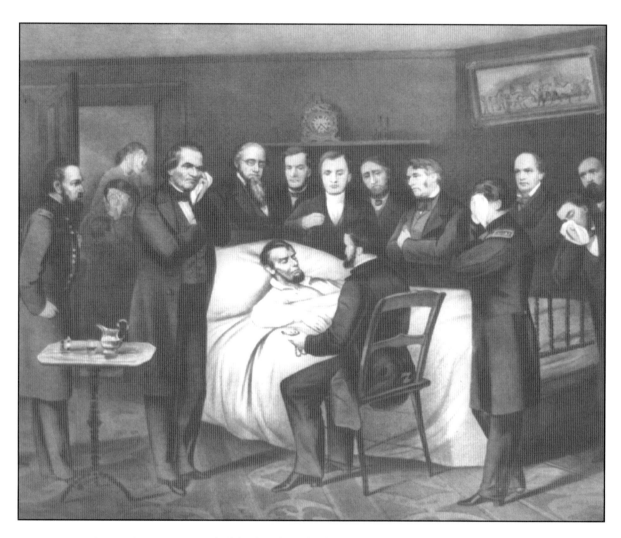

Lincoln is surrounded by his family, friends, and advisers at the time of his death.

President Lincoln was taken from the theater to a boarding house across the street. Family and friends stayed by his side during the night. The President died the next morning. He was 56 years old.

Lincoln began his presidency fighting to keep the Union together. He guided Americans through a terrible war and supported an amendment that would end slavery in America. In December 1865, the Thirteenth Amendment became law, and four million African Americans were freed.

AMERICAN TREASURES

Lincoln wrote two copies of his Emancipation Proclamation in his own hand, the preliminary copy read in September and the final copy read in January.

After Lincoln's death, the New York State Legislature bought the preliminary copy for $1,000. It was given to the State Library in Albany, New York. The State Library, part of the Capitol building, was destroyed in a fire in 1911, but the Emancipation Proclamation was saved. An employee of the State Department rescued it from the flames. The

preliminary copy is now kept at the new State Library in Albany.

The Chicago Historical Society acquired Lincoln's final copy, but it was destroyed in the Chicago fire of 1871. The five-page *signed* Emancipation Proclamation is kept at the National Archives in Washington, D.C.

President Lincoln writing his Emancipation Proclamation

TIME LINE

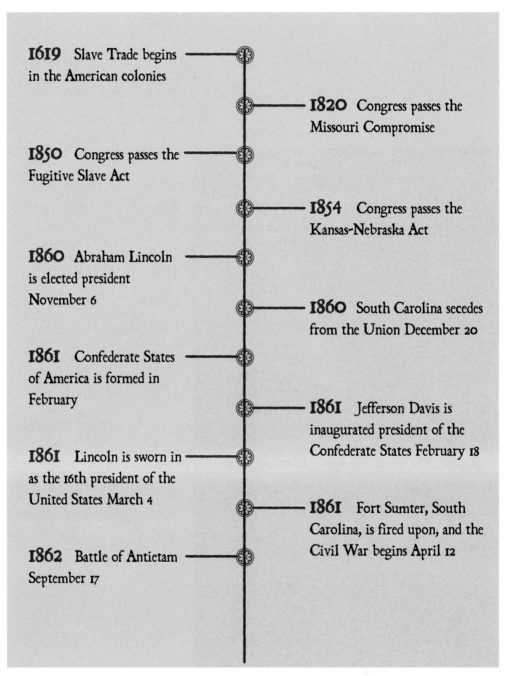

1619 Slave Trade begins in the American colonies

1820 Congress passes the Missouri Compromise

1850 Congress passes the Fugitive Slave Act

1854 Congress passes the Kansas-Nebraska Act

1860 Abraham Lincoln is elected president November 6

1860 South Carolina secedes from the Union December 20

1861 Confederate States of America is formed in February

1861 Jefferson Davis is inaugurated president of the Confederate States February 18

1861 Lincoln is sworn in as the 16th president of the United States March 4

1861 Fort Sumter, South Carolina, is fired upon, and the Civil War begins April 12

1862 Battle of Antietam September 17

1862 Lincoln delivers his preliminary Emancipation Proclamation September 22

1863 Lincoln delivers his final Emancipation Proclamation January 1

1865 General Lee surrenders to General Grant April 9. The Civil War ends

1865 Lincoln is assassinated and dies April 15

1865 Thirteenth Amendment becomes law in December

GLOSSARY

abolitionists (AB uh LISH eh nests) — people who want to do away with slavery

amendment (uh MEND muhnt) — a change made to a law

compromise (KOM pruh mize) — to agree to accept something that is not exactly what is desired

Emancipation Proclamation (i MAN si pay shuhn   PRAK leh MAY shuhn) — President Lincoln's formal announcement, which freed slaves living in Confederate States

emigrants (EM uh grents) — people who leave their home country to live in another one

fugitive (FYOO juh tiv) — someone who has run away from the law

indentured servants (in DEN chured SER vents) — people who are under contract to work for another over a long period of time

petitioned (peh TISH uhnd) — having made a formal written request

plantation (plan TAY shuhn) — a large farm in a warm climate

restitution (RES teh TOO shuhn) — a sum of money paid to a rightful owner

seceded (si SEED ud) — formally withdrawn from a group or organization

FURTHER READING

Holford, David M. *Lincoln and the Emancipation Proclamation.*
Enslow Publishers, 2002.

Martin, Michael J. *Emancipation Proclamation: Hope of Freedom for the Slaves.* Capstone Press, 2003.

Murray, Aaron R. *Civil War Battles and Leaders.*
Dorling Kindersley Publishing, 2004.

WEBSITES TO VISIT

www.historyplace.com/civilwar/
www.historyplace.com/lincoln/
www.americancivilwar.info/

ABOUT THE AUTHORS

David and Patricia Armentrout have written many nonfiction books for young readers. They have had several books published for primary school reading. The Armentrouts live in Cincinnati, Ohio, with their two children.

INDEX